Learning Field Hockey

This book was given to me by: _____

*Here you can
put a photo of yourself.*

My name: _____

My birthday: _____

My address: _____

_____

LEARNING FIELD HOCKEY

Katrin Barth &
Lutz Nordmann

Sports Science Consultant:
Dr. Berndt Barth

Meyer & Meyer Sport

Original Title: Ich lerne Hockey
© Aachen: Meyer & Meyer, 2005
Translated by Petra Haynes
AAA Translation, St. Louis, Missouri, USA
www.AAATranslation.com

British Library Cataloguing in Publication Data
A catalogue record for this book is available from the British Library
Learning Field Hockey
Katrin Barth / Lutz Nordmann
Oxford: Meyer & Meyer Sport (UK) Ltd., 2007
ISBN-10: 1-84126-210-2
ISBN-13: 978-1-84126-210-9
Aachen, Adelaide, Auckland, Budapest, Graz, Johannesburg,
New York, Olten (CH), Oxford, Singapore, Toronto
 Member of the World
Sports Publishers' Association (WSPA)
www.w-s-p-a.org
Printed and bound by: B.O.S.S Druck und Medien GmbH, Germany
ISBN-10: 1-84126-210-2
ISBN-13: 978-1-84126-210-9
E-Mail: verlag@m-m-sports.com

TABLE OF CONTENTS

Please note:
The exercises and practical suggestions in this book have been carefully chosen and reviewed by the authors. However, the authors are not liable for accidents or damages of any kind incurred in connection with the content of this book.

YOU WILL OFTEN SEE PICTURES OF ELO THE ELEPHANT IN THIS BOOK.

Pretty tricky! Sometimes Elo has a task or a riddle for you. You will find these next to the question mark. The answers and solutions are at the end of the book.

Here, Elo the elephant is giving you a tip or some important advice so you can do even better.

Next to this picture you will find exercises you can do outside of your regular training sessions. Maybe your friends, parents or siblings will participate in your additional training.

Wherever you see Elo with a pencil there is something for you to record, fill out or color.

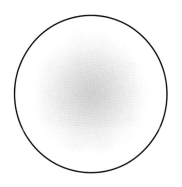

You can use this hockey book like a diary. Record your progress and your goals.

When you have become an experienced player, you can enjoy reading about how it all began. If you like you can add photos of yourself and your team, or collect autographs.

You will find a "blank" hockey ball next to some important techniques and special exercises. Once you have mastered the technique pretty well or have completed the suggested exercise, you can reward yourself by coloring the hockey ball with your favorite colors.

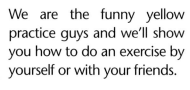

If you want, you can try it out right now on this first ball!

We are the funny yellow practice guys and we'll show you how to do an exercise by yourself or with your friends.

Once you have tried something, color the blank ball.

And I am the little blue mistake guy. I deliberately make mistakes – only to help you, of course! Let's see if you can recognize them all. If you're not sure, check the solution pages.

Elo loves ball games but he can't decide which ball sport to choose. Which sports do you recognize in this picture?

Do you know any other sports with a ball? Write them down here!

_____

_____

. . . . 1 DEAR BEGINNING HOCKEY PLAYER

You are probably one of those ball-crazy kids who can't come across a ball without wanting to play with it. There's an itch in your legs and you immediately want to chase after the ball, play it or put it in the goal. Sometimes it is a cute little bouncy ball, a brightly colored rubber ball or a tennis ball. It's just plain fun!

But it's even more fun when there are other children around and you can pass the ball to each other, make up games and rules and fight for victory.

Is that how you became interested in hockey? Or was it your friends, your parents or your siblings, who gave you hockey fever and got you excited? Do they already play for a club? Or maybe you got the idea to learn to play hockey from watching hockey games on television. In any case, you have chosen a great sport that is very popular all around the world.

Here are a few reasons why children like to play hockey. Which ones apply to you? Check "yes" or "no"!

	Yes	No
I enjoy running around and playing sports.	☐	☐
I like being with other children.	☐	☐
I want to play on a team.	☐	☐
I am already very involved in sports.	☐	☐
I am fast and therefore probably well suited.	☐	☐
I have a good feel for the ball.	☐	☐
I can handle the stick well.	☐	☐
I like watching hockey games.	☐	☐
My friends also play hockey.	☐	☐
I want to be better than the others.	☐	☐
I want to be among the best in my country.	☐	☐
I want to be really famous some day.	☐	☐

If you have answered most of these questions with "yes," you have chosen the right sport.

Many girls and boys learn to play hockey in a club. They practice regularly, play on teams and compete against other teams. But you don't have to be a member of a club to play hockey. Get a ball, a stick and an open space, add a few friends and you're ready to play!

In this hockey book we have listed some things of interest about your favorite sport. We explain the most important techniques, how to practice them and which mistakes to avoid. You will get numerous suggestions for practicing alone or with friends. There are also many game ideas to try out. Of course, Mom, Dad, your grandparents, siblings and anyone who – like you – enjoys it, is invited to practice.

Someday you may be a super-successful player at the national level or the top player on a successful team. But even if hockey remains a recreational sport on the field or indoors, you will notice how much you get out of this sport.

Whom do you most like to play hockey with? List the names here or collect signatures.

You will learn to play together with others, to become part of a team and to assert yourself. You will meet many interesting people and be part of the large "hockey family." You will learn to fight and develop willpower. You won't always be the glorious winner. You will also learn to deal with defeat, botched shots on goal, bad passes or receiving the ball badly. And soon you will notice that playing hockey regularly gives you more endurance, makes you more athletic and stronger, and keeps your body fit and healthy.

This little book is intended to be your companion as you learn to play hockey. If we ever explain something differently from the way your coach, trainer or an experienced player explains it, which can sometimes happen, then just ask questions. Even in hockey, opinions sometimes differ.

When we refer to trainers, coaches, hockey players, referees, etc., we of course are not just talking about men and boys, but also about all women and girls.

Have fun playing hockey!
The authors and Elo the elephant.

Elo's great-great-great-grandfather is playing hockey against his mirror image. But 10 differences have crept into the drawing on the right. Can you find them?

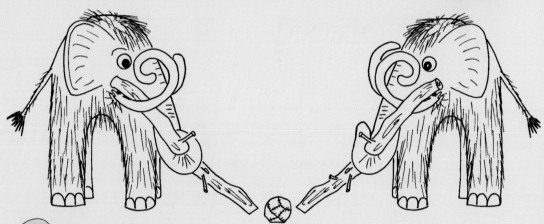

What are the ancestors of today's elephants called? Write down the beginning letters of the items below and you will be able to read it!

. .2 HOW FIELD HOCKEY BEGAN

The ball has certainly always been people's favorite piece of sports and play equipment. But no one really knows how ball games really began. But it was definitely so long ago that there were no videotapes, no photos, not even books. But researchers discovered ancient cave drawings depicting people playing with something ball-like.

There were the funniest ways of playing, using the hand, the head or the foot to play with the ball. Stone age people used staffs as sticks and the Native Americans had a game in which the ball was received and passed with the behind.

Many different sports have evolved from those wild ball games of ancient times to the present day. You have already found and listed a number of these on page 10.

DID YOU KNOW ...

... THAT FIELD HOCKEY IS PROBABLY THE OLDEST KNOWN GAME THAT USES A BALL AND STICK?

... THAT EVEN A LONG TIME AGO, THE CHINESE, PERSIANS AND AZTECS HAD GAMES USING STICKS AND BALLS?

... THAT AN OLD GRAVE PAINTING DEPICTING A TYPE OF HOCKEY GAME WAS DISCOVERED IN AFRICA? IT IS APPROXIMATELY 6000 YEARS OLD.

... THAT IN THE PAST, NATIVE AMERICANS WOULD HAVE AS MANY AS 50 PLAYERS ON A TEAM? THE PLAYER SCORING THE MOST GOALS RECEIVED GIFTS. THE GAME WAS NOT JUST ABOUT SCORING GOALS, BUT ALSO ABOUT INCAPACITATING THE OPPONENT.

... THAT MORE THAN 800 YEARS AGO,
A GAME CALLED "HOQUET" WAS PLAYED IN FRANCE.
THE ENGLISH NAME "HOCKEY" PROBABLY STEMS FROM THAT WORD.

... THAT IN THE PAST, IN SCOTLAND, IRELAND OR
WALES, THE GAME WAS OFTEN PLAYED WITH JUST A HOLE,
A CIRCLE OR A LINE SERVING AS THE "GOAL"?

... THAT ACCORDING TO THE OLD RULES, PLAYERS
WERE ALLOWED TO HIT THE BALL THROUGH THE AIR?
OCCASIONALLY A PLAYER DID GET HIT BY THE BALL.

... THAT MODERN HOCKEY DEVELOPED
APPROXIMATELY 200 YEARS AGO IN ENGLAND? THE
FIRST HOCKEY CLUB WAS ALSO FOUNDED THERE.

... THAT THE GAME HAS BEEN PLAYED
ON ARTIFICIAL TURF SINCE THE 70S.

... THAT THE FIRST INDOOR HOCKEY WORLD
CHAMPIONSHIPS WERE HELD IN 2003? THEY TOOK
PLACE IN LEIPZIG, GERMANY.

How many old balls are hidden on the two previous pages? Make a guess before you look and count. Write down that number first and then count.

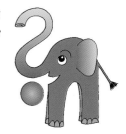

Write the number you guessed here:

Write the number you counted here:

FIELD HOCKEY IS A TEAM SPORT

In hockey, two teams are always competing against each other in a game, shooting goals and winning. Eventually, permanent teams were formed, clubs were founded and championships were held.

What is the name of your club?

_____

You can paste or draw your club's logo here.

Write down the name of the national field hockey association in your country:

_____

Put the logo of your field hockey association here.

NATIONAL CHAMPIONSHIPS

The men's and women's teams play for the national championships. The champions are determined at the end of the season.

Year	National Men's Champion

Year	National Women's Champion

Here you can keep a list of champions. Record the most recent data. Write the year in the left column and the team in the right column. Begin with the current year.

PICTOGRAM

Perhaps you have seen different sports depicted as drawings or symbols on television, in the newspaper, on stickers or posters. These symbols are called *pictograms*. The drawing is very simple, yet everyone immediately recognizes the sport it represents. Artists constantly create new symbols for big competitions and events.

This is a pictogram for field hockey.

How would you illustrate hockey using very simple lines? Here is a place for your ideas!

HAVE YOU HAD A LAUGH TODAY?

AN ELEPHANT AND A MOUSE ARE PLAYING HOCKEY.
THE ELEPHANT ACCIDENTALLY STEPS ON THE MOUSE'S FOOT.
"OOPS! I AM SO SORRY," SAYS THE ELEPHANT.
"NO PROBLEM," SAYS THE MOUSE.
"THAT COULD HAVE HAPPENED TO ME, TOO!"

AN ELEPHANT AND A MOUSE ARE WALKING IN THE HOT SUN.
THE ELEPHANT IS WALKING IN FRONT OF THE MOUSE
SO SHE CAN WALK IN HIS SHADOW. FINALLY THE ELEPHANT
SAYS, "YOU HAVE BEEN WALKING IN MY SHADOW FOR SO LONG,
NOW IT'S YOUR TURN TO GIVE ME SOME SHADE!"

A MOUSE SITS IN THE BLEACHERS WATCHING A HOCKEY GAME.
SUDDENLY, AN ELEPHANT ARRIVES AND SITS DOWN RIGHT IN FRONT OF
HER. THE MOUSE SQUEAKS, "I CAN'T SEE NOW!"
THE ELEPHANT DOESN'T REACT.
THE MOUSE SQUEAKS AGAIN, "I CAN'T SEE!"
STILL, THERE IS NO REACTION FROM THE ELEPHANT.
ANGRILY THE MOUSE GETS UP AND SITS IN FRONT OF THE ELEPHANT
AND SAYS: "NOW YOU CAN SEE FOR YOURSELF
HOW BAD THE VIEW IS WHEN SOMEONE SITS RIGHT IN FRONT OF YOU!"

AN ELEPHANT IS ENJOYING A SWIM IN THE LAKE.
A MOUSE WALKS UP AND SAYS, "QUICK! GET OUT OF THE WATER!"
THE ELEPHANT DOESN'T FEEL LIKE GETTNG OUT AND CONTINUES HIS SWIM.
THE MOUSE SHOUTS AGAIN, EXCITEDLY, "PLEASE, GET OUT! IT'S IMPORTANT!"
THE ELEPHANT GETS OUT OF THE WATER AND THE MOUSE SAYS,
"OKAY! YOU CAN GET BACK IN.
I JUST WANTED TO MAKE SURE
YOU WERE WEARING SWIMMING TRUNKS."

. . . . 3 HI THERE, TIMO WESS!

Timo Weß
Born July 2, 1982 in Moers, Germany
Player on the German national field hockey team, European Champion,
World Champion, bronze medalist at the 2004 Olympics in Athens

Hi there, Timo! What do you think is so great about field hockey?

It is a very appealing and fast sport. But yet almost anyone – young or old – can play hockey. The sport is really fun as a recreational activity and as a performance sport. You don't have to be particularly big, strong or fast because every player can compensate with skill and good technique.

What makes hockey special?

Hockey players in a club are part of a big family. They train together, everyone can play on a team, you make friends quickly and you are part of a great community.

How did you get started playing hockey?

I held a hockey stick for the first time at the home of some friends of my parents when I was six years old. Then I participated hockey at school and later signed up at the club in my hometown. At the same time, I was a pretty good soccer player, and for a long time I could not choose between the two sports. But soon I became more successful in hockey and finally stayed with it.

Do you sometimes not feel like practicing?

I think that happens to everyone. But when I have a goal, I can motivate myself very quickly. I want to help my team, play and score goals. For that I have to train well. Being at the Olympics was the best, and it made all of the hard training worthwhile.

Now you are already a European Champion, World Champion and have won the bronze medal at the 2004 Athens Olympics. Why do you keep going?

I ask myself that question sometimes. But I am hungry for bigger challenges and the next competitions. My biggest goal is to be part of the 2008 Olympics, to strengthen my team and be successful together.

But titles are not the most important thing. I enjoy hockey and have many friends amongst my teammates and opponents. What's great is that we often get to travel to other countries for international games and tournaments, and I get to see so much of the world.

What does hockey mean to you?

I enjoy the success and am happy when the strenuous training pays off. That kind of staying power also helps me with my studies. Besides, I have made great friends who help me whenever there are problems. I can definitely count on them.

But the sport isn't everything there is to life. A good education was always important to me and I am now working on my MBA degree. You cannot make a living on field hockey, which is why a good education and job are very important.

Which abilities must a young hockey player have?

Of course you need a good feel for the stick and ball. But endurance, flexibility and good technique are also important.

What is your advice to young athletes?

Take training seriously, but don't be overly persistent.

How can I get your autograph?

You can get autographs from the German Hockey Association (Deutscher Hockey-Bund).

Thank you very much for the interview and lots of luck in the future!

27

FANPAGE

My favorite player:

....

....

....

Photo

My favorite team:

....

....

Here you can collect autographs from players.

Here is a place for photos of you or your team.

........4 NO PAIN, NO GAIN

Surely you have dreamed about what it would be like to be the best. Everyone cheers you on, is in awe of you and admires you. The most successful clubs want you on their team. The fans assail you and want your autograph. You are deadly and tops in defense. Almost every opponent loses to you in a one-on-one duel; your dribbling technique and accurate passes are amazing.

Your teammates, your coach, your fans, your friends and parents, all congratulate you …

But stop! Laying in the grass dreaming of success isn't enough!

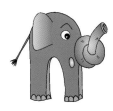

If you want to be a good hockey player, maybe even better than the others, you have to practice often and diligently. That's not always easy and isn't always fun right away.

Diligence leads to success!

GOALS

When you begin to play hockey, you will need to answer the following questions:

1 What is my goal?

2 What do I need to reach my goal?

3 How can I reach my goal?

1 What is my goal? Why do I practice so much?

Just playing the ball back and forth is fun. But soon you'll likely wish you could guide the ball more confidently, make better passes and especially score goals. Your friends should pick you for their team because you play so well and reliably. Maybe you want to finally play on a good club team or as a starter move up to a higher division. What would it be like to be discovered by a coach for the National Field Hockey League and play for a top club? Of course, you are still too young for that. Nevertheless, you should already have bigger goals today. You have to know what you want. If you don't have a goal, practicing will soon lose its fun. Continue to set higher goals for yourself. That's what the successful players have done.

Why do you want to learn to play hockey? Write down your goals here!

2 What do I need to reach my goal?

Of course, now you are going to ask what you can do to improve your performance. Definitely play lots and lots of hockey! Add to that the necessary exercises for improving the feel of the stick and ball, technique training, as well as endurance and strength training, which the hockey trainer will do with you. There will probably be some things you won't enjoy very much. Some things may seem boring and much too strenuous. But you must always remember that these exercises will help you reach your goal.

3 How can I reach my goal?

How are things going now that you continue to improve with regular practice? As long as the exercises are easy and relaxed the muscles will only do what they already know. Only when something is strenuous and the movements are no longer so easy are the muscles being strengthened. So you have to work hard and put some strain on your body to make progress. When you haven't been to hockey practice for a while, you will notice that you have gotten a little worse and are a little winded. Now you have to catch up!

The more diligently and frequently you practice, the better you will be!

PHYSICAL FITNESS IS IMPORTANT

WHAT'S WRONG WITH YOU, ELA? ARE YOU TIRED ALREADY? WE'VE ONLY BEEN PLAYING FOR HALF AN HOUR!

I'M EXHAUSTED!

Oh dear! What's wrong with Ela? After playing hockey for an hour with Elo she is so exhausted that she can barely stand up. Has that ever happened to you? Do you also get winded easily and lose your strength quickly? Then you need to work on your fitness level!

What should a good hockey player be able to do? Cross out the things that are not as important. If we forgot anything, write it down!

Play the flute

Run fast　　　　*Control the ball well*

Jump well

Ski　　*Play sports for an hour*

Be observant　　　*Tell jokes well*

What is physical fitness?

When playing hockey, you need to always be alert, chase the ball often and quickly, push the ball and hit it with lots of power. Can you do that for long? If so, then you are probably pretty fit. If not, the game won't be very fun for long, so you should work on improving your fitness level. You do that primarily by practicing regularly.

What you need

You need endurance to handle physical exertion for an extended period of time. Then you won't get winded so easily when running, jumping, bicycling or swimming. When it does get strenuous, you will quickly recover and feel fit again.

If you want to be able to stay in hockey position for a whole game or break into a run quick as lightning, you need strong leg muscles. Strength in your arms and hands is also important so you can hit the ball with power, receive it reliably and pass it on quickly.

For a hockey player, it is also important to be able to chase the ball quickly or instantly switch from forehand to backhand. For that, you need speed and dexterity.

To accurately play a ball or to stop it, you have to bend down very low. Also, to skillfully play the ball around the opponent in a one-on-one duel you will need flexibility.

At practice, you won't just chase after the ball with the stick in your hand. Your trainer will play a number of other ball games with you, as well as have you do exercises and calisthenics.

Participate in everything because all of these things will help improve your physical fitness level.

THIS IS HOW YOU CAN PRACTICE

Move!

- *Jogging*
- *Bicycling*
- *Skateboarding*
- *Swimming*
- *Playing basketball*
- *Playing soccer*
- *Skiing*
- *Hiking*

... and much more.

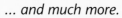

Fast and agile

- *Slalom run*
  Set up a slalom course using poles, cones or other objects. Who can get the fastest time without making a mistake?

- *High and low*
  Set up a course with several low hurdles in a row. The runner jumps over the first hurdle, crawls under the next hurdle, jumps over the next one, etc. Who gets the best time?

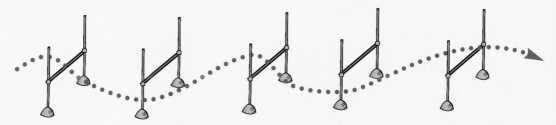

Balance and dexterity

- *Balancing*
  Balance on a chalk line or a beam. You may find low walls in your neighborhood or fallen trees in the forest to balance on.

- *Dexterity exercises*
  Many athletic exercises require dexterity and skill.
  Try inline skating, ice skating, walking on stilts, riding a mountain bike or bicycle. Have you ever juggled?

Which sport do you like to play besides hockey?
Write it down here.

HEY YOU! STOP CLOWNING AROUND!
WE NEED THAT CONE
FOR OUR SLALOM COURSE!

*Anyone who works hard
is allowed to occasionally
"clown around"!*

. .5 FIELD HOCKEY EQUIPMENT

Even a beginning hockey player wants to look like a real hockey player.

But what does that take?

Of course a jersey in the club colors and a number and name on the back, along with matching pants or skirt and socks in the appropriate color can make you look like a hockey player.

And while all of that looks great, in the beginning, it isn't really necessary. You can wear anything to play hockey. It must be comfortable and can't interfere with your playing. For indoor hockey, it is important to have the right shoes with non-skid soles. They should offer good support when running. You should wear shin guards under your socks to protect your shins from bruises.

When you play for a club, the teams are given uniforms for their games.

Oh boy! What a mess! How many sticks are in this pile?

Only two hockey sticks are identical. They are not all pointing in the same direction. Can you find them anyway?

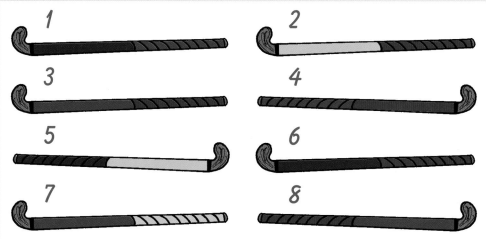

1
2
3
4
5
6
7
8

THE STICK

If you want to try out playing hockey, you can just wear your normal clothes. A tennis ball or a small rubber ball will work fine as a ball. You can play in the yard, on the street or on a sports field, and if you want to shoot at a goal, you can create one with two objects or draw a line.

There is only one thing you cannot substitute: You need a hockey stick to play hockey! A straight stick or a staff just won't work, because the special shape of a hockey stick is important for playing the game.

What does a hockey stick look like?

A hockey stick is made of wood or plastic. There are very simple sticks for school sports or for beginners to practice with. But there are also expensive and valuable sticks that were made specifically for individual players.

Every stick consists of:

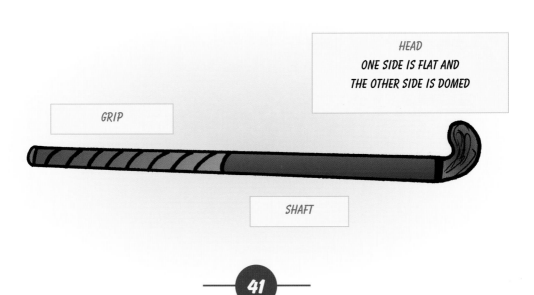

HEAD
ONE SIDE IS FLAT AND
THE OTHER SIDE IS DOMED

GRIP

SHAFT

Many hockey players also say shinny instead of hockey stick. Although that is a correct term, in this book we have to choose one term. So we will stick with hockey stick. You and your trainer can decide what you want to call it.

Shape, size and weight

A hockey stick is up to 40 inches long. Of course, there are shorter ones for smaller players and for children. The weight also varies. It ranges from 17 to 24 ounces. Size and weight limits are specified in the regulations.

This is how a hockey stick is used

The hockey stick is used to play the ball – to guide it, to receive the ball, to pass it, and especially to shoot goals. The ball can only be played with the flat side, which is why that side is always turned towards the ball.

Of course, the stick is not used to drive back an opponent or knock him down.

THE BALL

What would a hockey game be without the ball? All of the players chase after this little sphere and want to put it in the opposing goal, no matter what.

Material and size of a hockey ball

The ball is made of white or colored synthetic material. The balls measure approximately 9 inches around and weigh 5 1/2 to 5 3/4 ounces.

This is how the ball is played

The ball is hit, pushed, shoved, bounced or flicked with the stick. It can even briefly be stopped with the hand on the ground or in the air.

But you cannot play or flick the ball dangerously high. You can also not slice the ball in such a way that it flies erratically. The ball cannot be carried, thrown, held, or stopped or kicked with the foot.

THE CLOTHES

To play hockey, you should wear comfortable and practical clothes. Depending on the weather that includes long or short pants and shirt. The tennis shoes should fit well and lend good support for fast sprints and quick ball handling. The team has uniforms for games. Those include jerseys with a number on the back, shorts for boys and skirts for girls, and matching socks.

PROTECTIVE GEAR

Hockey is a fair sport played by definite rules. The referee makes sure the rules of the game are adhered to. Many players especially like the fact that in hockey the players have little physical contact, but rather just play the ball with the stick.

Even so, there is that odd stray ball or the stick can get in the way, which can be painful. That is why the field players have special protective gear. You are young and need a complete set of healthy teeth for a long time to come. Protect them with a mouth guard. Your shins are always in the danger zone due to the sticks and the low-flying ball. That is why you should wear shin guards under your socks. In indoor hockey, the players wear a knuckle guard on the left hand.

THE GOALIE GEAR

A goalie plays a very important position. He must keep his goal "clean," meaning he has to prevent the other team from scoring a goal. To do this, he must always be alert, react quickly, and he especially shouldn't be afraid of the balls.

Of course, not being afraid isn't always that easy. The ball is hard and sometimes approaches the goal at a high speed. In this situation, the goalie has to stop the ball with his stick and his body. For that, he has special goalie gear that protects him but also allows him to move around easily.

This includes:

- Helmet with cage and throat protector
- Chest protector or cup
- Goalie pants
- Goalie pads
- Goalie kickers
- Glove for the stick hand and the catching hand

EVERYTHING PACKED?

You are very excited because you are going to an out-of-town game. You have practiced a lot and the team lineup is set.

But imagine you arrive at the game location, unpack your gym bag and ... where are the shoes? Your well-broken in super running shoes are at home – far away! Just plain forgotten! There is no one to borrow shoes from and they wouldn't fit you properly anyway.

The fact that you can't play now is not only irritating to you, but it is also a big problem for your team.

Your parents could of course help pack your bag, but every player is responsible for his own complete and clean equipment!

THE CHECKLIST

Many athletes know that anxious feeling of forgetting something for an important match or tournament. That is why it is important to prepare everything early. Pack your gym bag the night before so you can go to bed with your mind at ease.

Many athletes have found making a checklist to be useful. You write down everything you want to bring along. Anything that's packed is checked off. Use a pencil so you can erase the checks for the next time you pack.

These things also belong in your gym bag. Did we forget anything? Draw it or write it down here!

Fruit for a snack.

Water or juice and water mix.

Shower items.

After sweating and showering, a hat is very important on colder days.

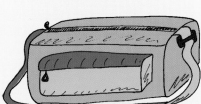

Your good luck charm.

Hockey players need warm muscles. That is why they often wear warm-up suits before the game and during breaks to keep from getting chilled.

Sometimes just a few sweets are important.

MY CHECK LIST

☐ JERSEY

☐ SHORTS / SKIRT

☐ SOCKS

☐ SHIN GUARDS

☐ SHOES

☐ HOCKEY STICK

☐ SHOWER ITEMS

☐ _____

☐ _____

☐ _____

☐ _____

Use the blank lines to write down anything else you can't forget.

THE PLAYING FIELD

You can easily find a suitable place for playing hockey.
Suitable places are:

- the school gym
- the school yard
- a sports field
- a grassy backyard
- a special hockey field

The surface can be:

- parquet floor
- asphalt or a hard court
- grass
- well-maintained artificial turf

Maybe there will be two of you playing on one goal, or two teams on one goal, or it might be like a real hockey game with two teams and two goals.

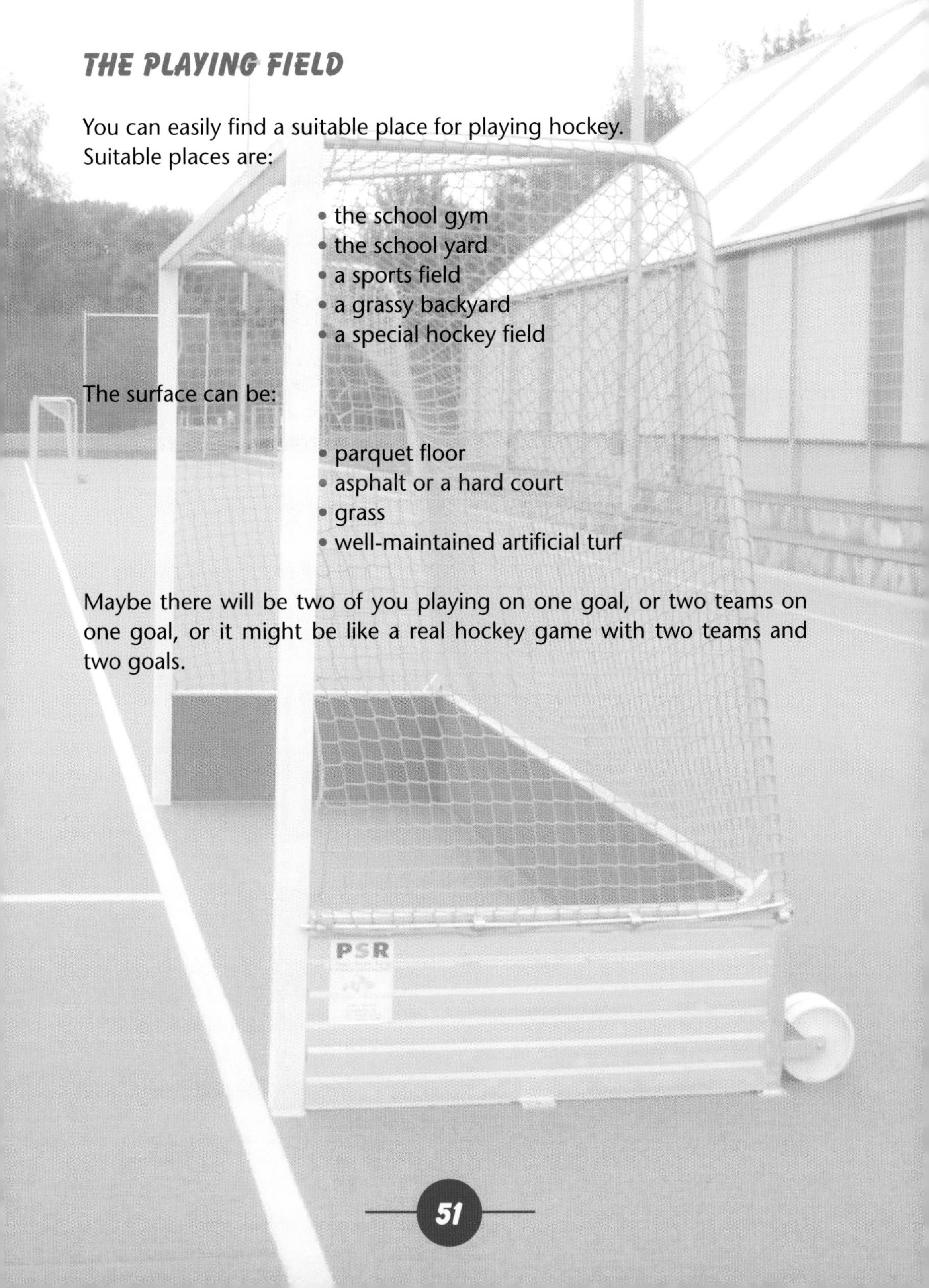

HOCKEY QUIZ

We have listed four possible answers to each question.

But only one of the four answers is correct. Can you find it?

1 What is another name for a hockey stick?

A	Staff	B	Shinny
C	Hammer	D	Club

2 What do the players call their shin protection?

A	Stockings	B	Shields
C	Boots	D	Guards

3 Where are hockey games played other than on a hockey field?

A	In a sports hall	B	In the forest
C	At the beach	D	At an indoor pool

4 What is a "head"?

A	A bad foul	B	A wild spectator
C	A part of the stick	D	A defeat

. . . . .6 A FEEL FOR STICK AND BALL

WHAT IS A FEEL FOR STICK AND BALL?

Is it the joy the ball feels when it flies through the air so high and fast?

Or is it the pain it feels from a hard hit with the stick?

Or is it maybe the feelings the hockey player has for his stick and ball?

A feel for stick and ball refers to how well a player can maneuver the ball with his stick. He feels how the ball rolls, how much strength he needs to push and hit the ball, and how the ball can be stopped. A good hockey player must have that feel.

Many sticks and one ball! Whoever handles the ball best on the field will win!

In a game, you have to control the ball. You receive your teammate's pass and swiftly pass it on. Then you move around the opponent, take the ball away from him and shoot directly into the goal. You're the boss, and you show the ball what's what!

At the same time, you have to react quickly. In hockey, the player is not allowed to catch the ball or hold on to it while thinking about how to proceed. He must make quick decisions and react fast as lightning. That can only be done with a good feel for the ball. You acquire this feel for stick and ball through lots and lots of practice.

Even the best hockey players continue to do exercises with stick and ball. It would be best if you made a little time for that every day. You will find exercises on the following pages.

Have fun!

EXERCISES FOR THE FEEL FOR STICK AND BALL

How can you practice?

While standing up, sitting on the floor, sitting on a chair. Take a ball and play with it.

Where can you practice?

You don't need much space for the exercises. You can practice outside in the park, in your backyard, and even inside as long as it doesn't disturb anyone. You just need to be careful not to break anything.

What can you practice with?

The stick and the ball are your toys. You can certainly try out different sticks and even use a tennis ball or a little rubber ball to practice with.

How fast do you have to be while you practice?

A player should be able to handle the ball with some speed. But that doesn't happen right away. First, you should do the exercises slowly and then try to do them a little faster each time. Later, your exercises should be accurate and fast.

WAYS YOU CAN PRACTICE

On these pages you will find some exercises for the feel for stick and ball. You can practice just about anywhere. Just make sure that nothing is damaged and no one is disturbed.

 ## Juggling

- *Juggle the ball with the flat side of your stick. How far can you count before it falls off? Who can go the longest?*
- *Juggle the ball with the flat side of your stick. How far can you walk while you juggle? Who can walk the farthest?*
- *Juggle the ball with the edge of the stick.*

- Once the juggling is going well, try to play the ball a couple of inches higher, (or even higher than that) and then catch it with the stick.

 ## Passing

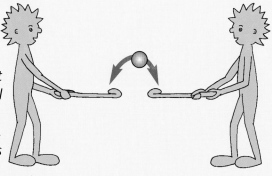

- *Two players face each other at a slight distance. Now the ball is played back and forth.*
- *Before the ball is passed back, the player juggles it with his stick.*

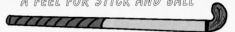

3 Rotating the stick

To switch from forehand to backhand, you rotate the stick. We provide a detailed description of this on page 64. The left hand rotates the stick, and the right hand provides support and control.

- *Play the ball in front of you with little touches from right to left.*

- *Play the ball slalom-like around small obstacles.*

4 At the target

Set up targets of varying shapes at various distances. Now try to hit all of the targets. Who will score the most hits? Observe which technique causes the ball to fly higher or hit most accurately.

Once you have tried an exercise and practiced it a few times, you can color the corresponding ball.

Write down how many times you practice in a week.

The week goes in the top row and every time you practice, draw a line underneath.

WEEK							
NUMBER	𝍸𝍸 /						

OH, NO!
WHAT HAPPENED TO MY ARMS?
MAYBE I PRACTICED TOO MUCH?

.........7 CONTROLLING, PASSING AND STOPPING THE BALL

What could be better in hockey than shooting a goal? Sometimes you do it with just a little flick or with an unstoppable bomb. You can swiftly dribble around your opponent and send the goalie into the wrong corner. The spectators are thrilled!

Maybe you will drive the other team to near desperation when you win every one-on-one duel, catch a bomb of a ball, reliably receive passes and make incredibly accurate passes to your teammates.

All of these successful actions are the result of diligent practice. For every situation, there are special techniques that need to be practiced again and again. It is important that you know the exact position of the stick, your body position and the position of your feet, and know how the movement is executed.

On the following pages, we have illustrated the most important movements for a beginning hockey player.

Which player is playing the ball to another teammate?

WHAT IT TAKES TO BE A GOOD HOCKEY PLAYER

For the game to be fun, a beginning hockey player must be good at handling the hockey stick and able to master basic situations.

That includes:

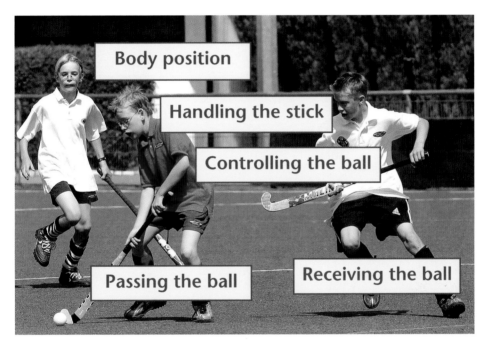

Body position

Handling the stick

Controlling the ball

Passing the ball

Receiving the ball

In this book, we describe the fundamental techniques for you. We show you what the technique looks like, what you have to pay attention to, how to practice and which mistakes can occur.

You learn best when your coach or another experienced hockey player shows you the technique and you can practice with the group. But once you are at home you can look over the illustrations and descriptions in this book at your leisure. You can do many of the exercises alone or with your parents, siblings or friends. Always make sure not to practice any mistakes! The pictures of mistakes will help you to recognize them so you can avoid or correct them.

THE BODY POSITION

During the time that people have been playing hockey, a particular body position has developed. This position allows the players to run fastest, control the ball best and pass most reliably.

At the ready

This is the position the player assumes when he is just following the game without chasing the ball. He is ready to run to the ball or receive a pass at any moment.

This is what you have to pay attention to:

- Erect body position.
- The feet are planted approximately hip-width apart.
- The stick is held with both hands, horizontally in front of the body.
- Follow the game closely.

Playing position

This is the position in which the player moves with the ball, receives the ball or passes it.

This is what you have to pay attention to:

- Low body position.
- The left hand is placed at the end of the stick.
- The right hand is placed several hand-widths below the left.
- The eyes should be taken off the ball as much as possible to keep track of the play, to find a teammate to pass to, or to find an open space or a goal opportunity.

The left hand holds the stick and performs the rotations. The right hand guides and stabilizes the stick.

THE STICK POSITION

In hockey, the stick is the most important instrument, and it acts like an extension of your arm. You must therefore handle it safely and skillfully. It should be held in such a way that it won't fly out of your hand but will follow the ball when you hit it a little bit harder. The hockey stick must also be maneuverable enough so you can quickly turn and move it. That is very important because the ball can only be played with the flat side of the stick.

The stick position

This is how the stick is held:

• The left hand is placed at the end of the stick or just below.

• The right hand holds the stick approximately three hand-widths below the left hand.

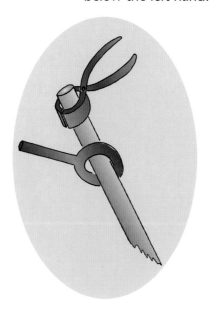

Rotating the stick

This is what you need to do in order to quickly move the stick from forehand to backhand and from backhand to forehand.

This is what you have to pay attention to:

• The left hand holds the stick and determines which way it will rotate – like tightening a screw with a pair of pliers.

• The right hand does not take part in rotating. It is like a grommet that guides the screw and makes sure it doesn't slip.

Forehand and backhand

Forehand position

This is what the hockey stick looks like in forehand position. The ball is to the left of the stick against the flat side.

Backhand position

For the backhand position, the ball is on the right side of the stick. But since the ball can only be played with the flat side of the stick, the stick must be rotated to the backhand. Now the head points down.

For the switch from forehand to backhand or backhand to forehand to be made very quickly, the rotary motion must be as small as possible. Practice by making many quick turns. Try taking your eyes off the ball as soon as possible.

The players are making mistakes with the body and stick position. Can you see them?

1

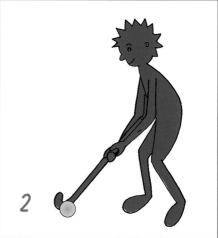

2

3

Which other mistakes do you have to watch out for? What does your trainer tell you? You can write it down here.

BALL CONTROL

Carrying the ball forehand at the side of the body

In order to move the ball and carry it with you, you can carry it on your right side with the flat side of the stick. In doing so, you move the ball very close to the stick, or shinny it along with little taps.

It is a good way to move the ball fast, especially when you have a lot of space.

This is what you have to pay attention to:

- Knees and hip joints are slightly bent.
- The stick is held diagonally in front of the body.
- The stick surface points in the direction of travel.
- The back of the left hand also points in the direction of travel.
- The right hand is approximately three hand-widths below the left hand, and the back of the hand points to the body.
- Both wrists are flexed.
- The stick and the left forearm form a nearly straight line.

Protracted ball control

The ball is also carried on the right when carrying it protracted at the side of the body. But in doing so the ball is carried farther back, approximately level with the right foot. The stick is held closer to the ground and the ball is carried in the crook of the stick's head.

This allows you to cover the ball better and protect it from the opposing player.

This is what you have to pay attention to:

- The ball is level with the rear foot.
- The stick is tilted lower to the ground.
- The ball is "hooked" into the crook of the stick's head.
- The toes point in the direction of travel.
- The torso is turned towards the ball.

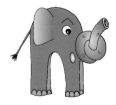

This technique makes it more difficult for the opponent to reach the ball.

Carrying the ball forehand in front of the body

With this technique, you don't carry the ball on the side but rather in front of the body. This also allows you to move very fast.

The stick stays on the ball, and you can quickly dribble around your opponent or pass to a teammate. This technique is used particularly on artificial turf or indoors.

This is what you have to pay attention to:

- The body is in a crouched position.
- The stick is held in front of the body.
- Because the stick is held differently, the arms are also more in front of the body.
- The ball is carried in a fluid motion without tapping it.

Stopping the ball

When carrying the ball on the side, it is important to also be able to stop the ball. That's what you have to do when the ball gets too fast, to change directions or to make a pass.

This is what you have to pay attention to:

- You slow down.
- The left foot is in front.
- The stick is rotated from forehand to backhand position over the ball.
- You make the rotation with your left hand. The stick is rotated in the relaxed right hand.
- The ball is stopped in front of the left toe.
- After the stop, immediately bring the forehand back behind the ball.

Carrying the ball forehand at the side while turning

To go around an obstacle – in a real game this would be your opponent – you need a special turning technique.

The left turn

- The ball is moved in front of the body at a run.
- The left elbow is close to the body.
- The right hand pushes forward.
- The flat side of the head points to the left front.
- The ball is played around the turn with continuous tapping.

The right turn

- You pass the ball.
- The left elbow moves to the front.
- The stick is tilted slightly downward.
- The left shoulder is dropped.
- The forearm and the stick form a line.
- The turn is executed with the ball at foot level.

Forehand-backhand ball control

This form of ball control is somewhat slower than the others. But it has the advantage of allowing you to quickly pass to the left or the right when dribbling. It is a way to easily trick an opponent when you want to dribble around him.

This is what you have to pay attention to:

- The legs are in a slight straddle position, and the ball is in front of the body.
- The stick surface is placed against the right side of the ball.
- The stick is held in a rotation grip as described on page 64.
- Only the left hand rotates the stick to the backhand position over the ball.
- Now the head points down and the flat side is placed against the left side of the ball.
- As the ball is carried, it is played with the forehand to the left front and with the backhand to the right front.

First practice this movement standing, then at a walk, and later at a run. Make very small motions close to the ball. Taking big swings takes too much time and the opponent could quickly take the ball away from you.

The left wrist is rigid. The forearm, the hand and the stick form a straight line.

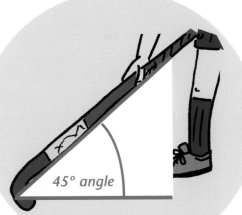

45° angle

This applies to all forms of ball control:

The hockey stick is held at an approximate 45° angle to the floor.

THIS IS HOW YOU CAN PRACTICE

*Good and reliable ball control requires lots of practice.
Here we have made up a few exercises for you.*

You can practice alone or with friends.

1 Moving the ball straight on

*Start out slow and with your eyes on the ball. Now try to occasionally take
your eyes off the ball and look ahead.*

- *Move the ball along a line.*
- *Designate a place that you will guide the ball to.*
- *Try to reach that designated place as fast as possible.*
- *Continue to look ahead to your destination as long as possible.*

2 Contests with ball control

- *Everyone is standing at the starting line. On command, everyone
  takes off at a run. Who reaches the designated place first?*
- *A referee stands at the finish line. During the race, he signs three
  numbers in a row with this fingers. Who saw all of the signs
  correctly while controlling the ball?*
- *Two players stand facing each other at a distance. Each one has a
  starting line. On command, they take off running and switch sides. Who
  gets to the other side first? Careful, don't collide!*

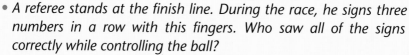

3 **Shadow**

One player runs ahead with a ball and the second player must follow his exact path with his ball against his stick. You can add in various turns and stops.

4 **Slalom course**

Set up a slalom course. Build in left turns, right turns and straight-aways.

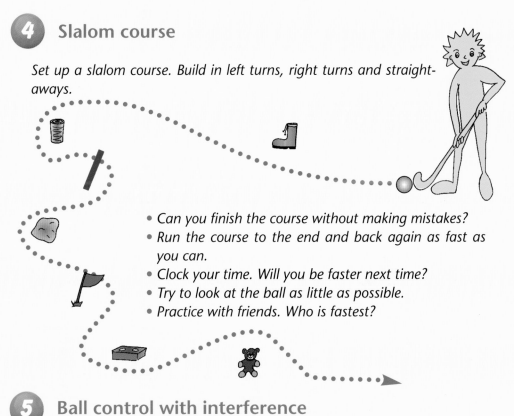

- Can you finish the course without making mistakes?
- Run the course to the end and back again as fast as you can.
- Clock your time. Will you be faster next time?
- Try to look at the ball as little as possible.
- Practice with friends. Who is fastest?

5 **Ball control with interference**

You can add these difficulties to many exercises.

- The "interferer" does not have a hockey stick and cannot touch you or the ball. He just continually stands in your way and you have to go around him.
- The "interferer" has a hockey stick and tries to use it to knock the ball away from you.
- You are switching sides again, but only one player has a ball. The other player tries to take it away during the switch and carry it across the finish line himself. Who will make it?

The players are making mistakes while controlling the ball. Can you find them?

Our assumption here is the ideal case scenario. But you already know that during a game you will occasionally have to deviate from that.

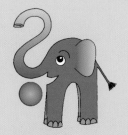

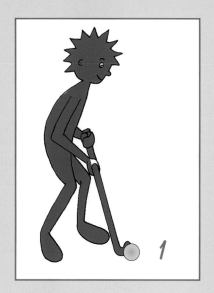

1

2

3

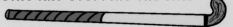

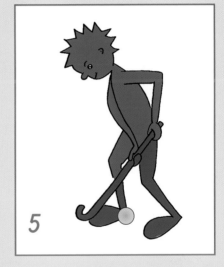

Check the mistake that you, too, have trouble with. But of course only with pencil so you can soon erase that check.

PASSING THE BALL

In a game, you just want to play the ball straight on, pass it to a teammate, execute a free hit and, most of all, score a goal.

The forehand push pass

The push pass in front of the body is a good way to pass the ball to a teammate over a short distance. If your teammate gets open and is in a favorable position, you can make a quick and accurate pass to him.

This is what you have to pay attention to:

• The left shoulder points in passing direction.
• Knees and hips are slightly bent.
• During the preliminary movement, the weight is on the right leg.
• During the pass, the weight is shifted more to the left leg.
• The hands push in passing direction.

The push pass from a lateral position

You get in a lateral position for the push pass when your passes have to cover longer distances.

This is what you have to pay attention to:

- The ball lies between the feet. It is far enough away from the body so the stick has a 45° angle.
- The ball leaves the stick approximately at the level of the left foot.
- The stick is swung in passing direction and is slowed down approximately at hip level.

To avoid the threat of injury, it is important that:
you slow the stick down when the ball leaves the stick.

Hitting

This is a technique that can only be used in field hockey. The ball is hit hard and can thus travel a long distance.

This is how you make a pass to a teammate, as well as a shot on goal, a free hit or a bully.

This is what you have to pay attention to:

- The right hand slides to the top of the stick, directly below the left hand.
- The body position is low.
- The legs are in a wide straddle position.
- During the swing, the stick swings back close to the ground.
- For the hit, the stick is quickly swung forward behind the ball.

In the beginning, when you practice, you should pay more attention to accuracy and less to power of impact. That will come later.

Do you have a photo of an exciting game sequence with your team? Paste it here. Of course, you can also draw a picture instead.

The backhand push pass

When a ball approaches on your right side, the fastest way to stop it is with a backhand maneuver. Then the ball can immediately be played back or passed on the right with a backhand push pass.

This is what you have to pay attention to:

- The player stands perpendicular to the ball.
- The left shoulder points in passing direction.
- The ball is in the center between the feet. It is far enough away that the angle of the stick is 45°.
- The stick is in backhand position with the flat side against the ball.
- The ball is played to the right with a vigorous stroke to the right.

THIS IS HOW YOU CAN PRACTICE

Good and reliable passing and successful shots on goal require a lot of practice. Here we have made up a few exercises for you. You can practice alone or with friends.

1 To the target

You mark a designated target area and pass the ball so it touches or stops within the marked area.

- Mark your designated targets at various distances.
- Who will get the most hits?
- Have someone play the ball to you. Receive it and immediately pass it to the designated target.

2 Practicing shots on goal alone

If you want to practice alone, you should plan it so you don't always have to chase after the ball by bringing extra balls.

- Play against a fallen tree trunk or set up a board. If you like you can mark a target with chalk or tape. Now try to hit this target from various distances and positions.

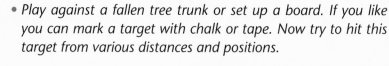

3 Passing

Two players stand facing each other and play the ball back and forth.

- *In the beginning, play so the other player can easily receive the ball.*
- *Slowly make it more difficult and play the ball harder or more laterally. Now the ball has to be chased.*

- *Alternate between the different types of passes.*
- *Change the distance or play through a goal.*

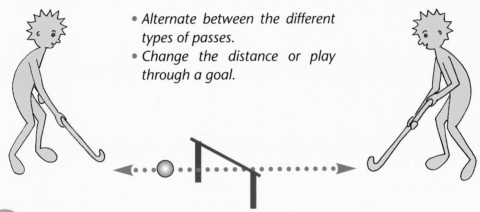

4 Practicing shots on goal

Every player has a goal he has to guard.
At the same time, he wants to take a successful shot on the other player's goal.

Once you have tried an exercise and practiced it a few times, you can color the corresponding ball.

These players are making mistakes with the push pass. Can you find them?

1

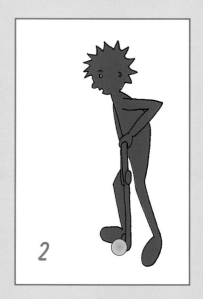

2

3

These players are making mistakes hitting the ball. Can you find them?

1

2

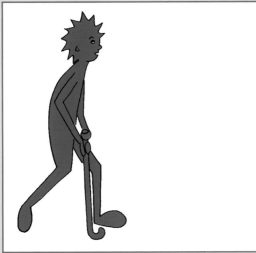

3

Check the mistake that you, too, have trouble with. But, of course, only with pencil so you can soon erase that check.

Oh no! I'm lost!

How will this player find the way to her team? Can you help?

RECEIVING THE BALL

A very important technique for team play is receiving the ball. Only the player who safely receives a pass from a teammate can make a successful play. But if, instead, the ball is continuously lost, the game soon won't be fun anymore.

Frontal forehand stopping

When stopping frontally, the player turns his body to the incoming ball, thus being able to watch it closely. For a beginner, this is the safest form of receiving the ball.

Frontal forehand stopping with low stick

If a ball rolls up slowly without bouncing, you can stop it with a low stick. This allows you to increase the width of the stopping surface. It is a good stopping technique, particularly for playing on artificial turf or indoors.

This is what you have to pay attention to:

- You turn your entire body toward the incoming ball.
- The stick is laid close to the ground.
- Make a roof!
- Stand still.

Hockey players also call this form of stopping "laying down a plank."

Wide stopping surface

When you hold the stick close to the ground you broaden the stopping surface. You can see what that means by the red triangle in the drawing. You will be able to stop the ball even if it rolls a little more to the left or to the right.

Make sure the gap above the ground is not too wide or the ball will roll under the stick!

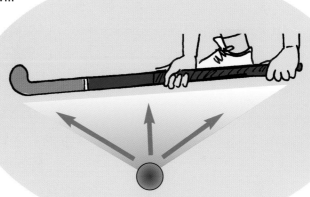

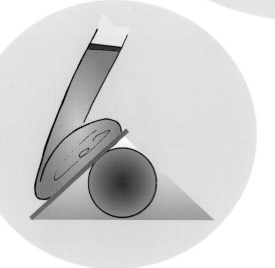

Building a roof

The stick is tilted forward slightly, in direction of the incoming ball. This forms a kind of roof over the ball and the ball cannot bounce over the stick.

Frontal forehand stopping with high stick

If a ball doesn't come in slowly but bounces towards you, you can stop it with a vertical stick in front of the body. You thereby expand the stopping surface upward.

This is what you have to pay attention to:

- Turn your entire body toward the incoming ball.
- The legs can be in a slight straddle position.
- Stand still.
- The stick stands up nearly straight on the ground in front of you.

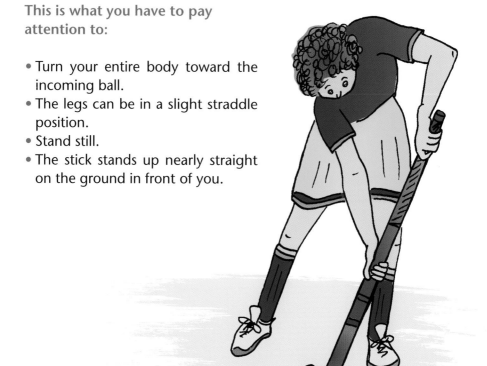

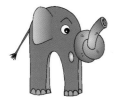

Hockey players also say:

The stick "sucks up" the ball.

High stopping surface

When an incoming ball bounces, you are not able to predict exactly how high it will be when it reaches your stick. If you hold the stick vertically, you can increase the height of the stopping surface.

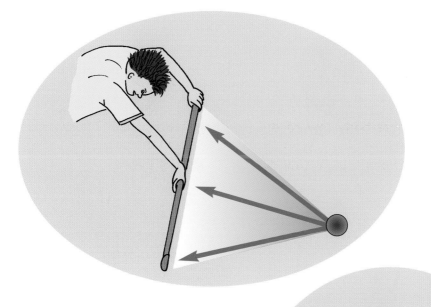

Building a roof

The top of the stick is tilted a little more in the direction of the incoming ball. This forms a kind of roof over the ball. That helps to stop the ball more securely and it can't bounce away as easily.

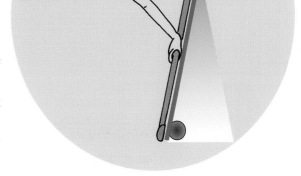

Lateral forehand stopping

You can also receive the ball in a lateral position. The advantage here is that after stopping the ball you can immediately carry out a forehand push pass or a forehand hit from this position.

This is what you have to pay attention to:

- The left shoulder points in the direction of the ball.
- The feet are parallel.
- The legs can be in a slight straddle position.
- You stand still.
- The stick stands at a 45° angle on the ground in front of you.
- Don't forget to "build a roof!"

To receive the **ball laterally with a backhand,** you switch from forehand to backhand. During the stick rotation, you get on the balls of your feet and turn your feet to the left. You receive the ball in this stride position on a level with the rear foot.

Stopping with low backhand

This way of receiving the ball is particularly advantageous indoors or for shallow balls on artificial turf. You can change the type of grip depending on how far the stick has to reach.

1. You can set the stick on the ground with both hands in backhand position.
2. If you want to reach a ball that is farther away, you should hold the stick at the top with only the left hand. This increases your reach.
3. In the drawing the player holds the stick with a short grip. He wants to stop the ball approximately on a level with his right foot.

This is what you have to pay attention to:

- Go into a deep knee bend.
- The stick lays on the ground in backhand position.
- You stand still.
- Don't forget to "build a roof!"

For a subsequent shot on goal, it is important that you quickly stand up and bring the forehand back behind the ball.

THIS IS HOW YOU CAN PRACTICE

Receiving the ball well and securely requires a lot of practice. Here we have made up a few exercises for you. You can practice alone or with friends.

1 Stop and back

Have someone play the ball to you. Receive it and immediately play it back again. At the same time, try not to change your foot position.

- *Receive vertically – forehand push pass.*
- *Receive low in forehand position – forehand push pass.*
- *Have someone play the ball to you. Receive it and immediately pass it to another marked target.*

2 Two playing back and forth

You and another player stand facing each other and play the ball back and forth.

- *Start fairly close together and then take a step back after each pass.*
- *First play so the other player can reach the ball easily, then occasionally play it a little to the left or to the right.*

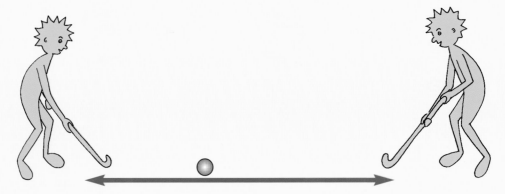

3 **Multiple players**

Several players stand in a circle and play the ball to each other. The ball is stopped and then passed on to the next player.

Hopefully, you have noticed that the passing exercises and the receiving exercises can't really be separated. They are closely connected. A ball must first be passed so you can receive it. And you will often pass the ball again after successfully receiving it. That's why all of the exercises help you train several things at the same time.

Continue to change the techniques when you are practicing. But, most of all, practice the things you are having trouble with.

These players are making mistakes receiving the ball. We have written them down.

Do you know what will happen if you make these mistakes when you receive the ball? Write it down!

The player doesn't tilt the stick forward but rather tilts it back.

This is what is likely to happen:

_____

_____

_____

_____

_____

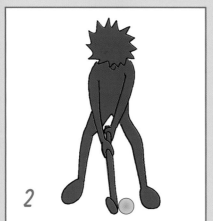

The player isn't "building a roof."

This is what is likely to happen:

_____

_____

_____

_____

_____

100

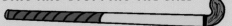

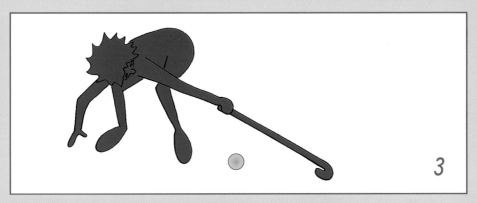

The player doesn't set the stick down on the ground.

This is what is likely to happen:

_____

_____

_____

This number four is a bonus question. Can you see which mistake the player is making?

DRIBBLING

Of course, no opponent will allow you to run the ball to the goal and possibly score a goal without opposition. The players on the opposing team will try to take the ball away from you. But you want to play the ball past the opponent, leaving him "in the dust," thus gaining a superior score. You can create a good chance for a goal like that.

This is how you dribble around the opponent

1 You bring the ball in position in front of the body. Now you have the option of playing in any direction. Watch your opponent closely and think about how to proceed.

2 You quickly play the ball past the opponent. In doing so you can also fake him out. Suggest a wrong direction and then dribble around him on the other side.

3 After dribbling around him, run away from the opponent as quickly as possible towards your target.

DEFENSE

If the opponent has possession of the ball, you want to take the ball away from him as fast as possible. Here, too, it is very important to have mastered the techniques for defense and ball control.

But you don't just want to interfere with the opponent, take the ball away from him and get it in your own possession, you also want to keep the ball. For that, you have to guide it securely, control it and not let it be immediately taken away again. Take advantage of this situation for your own successful attack.

This is how a successful defense is executed:

1 Gain possession of the ball.

2 Control the ball.

3 Start your own attack.

For a beginner, "laying down a plank" is the most often used and safest defensive technique.

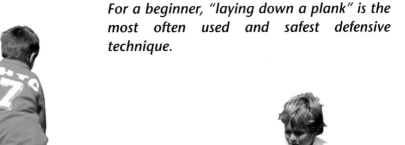

Ela is searching for her stick. Can you help her?

- The stick is yellow in the middle.
- The stick does not have a blue grip.
- The stick has two white stripes.
- The head of the stick is not the color of wood.

. . . . .8 KEEPING THINGS STRAIGHT

Almost everything in people's lives is regulated. What a mess it would be if everyone could just do whatever they wanted. Families have rules that everyone has to abide by, as do schools, day care, and sports teams. There are traffic rules for motorists, and every card game has rules.

It is the same in sports. Every sport has rules on how the sport is practiced, how a competition proceeds, and when a team wins or loses. There are also regulations for what is allowed and what is prohibited.

In hockey there is an entire book of rules. Thank goodness it is like that! Otherwise there would be a lengthy discussion about points and penalties after every action and no one would enjoy the game.

We don't want to write about all of the hockey rules here. That would be too difficult and not that important for you right now. When you play with friends, you can make your own rules, and at the club the trainer will explain the rules there.

If you are interested, you can read all about hockey regulations on-line at www.fihockey.org.

THE OFFICIAL RULES

When playing with your friends, you can play by your own rules. What matters is that you all agree, and that everyone accepts the rules and abides by them.

But it is still very important to know the actual hockey rules and regulations. You can fashion your "recreational" rules after them.

The teams

The nice thing about hockey is that it is a team sport. You play together with other athletes, you fight together, enjoy your victories and you are never alone when you lose. A field hockey team consists of 11 players (10 players and one goalie) and an indoor hockey team has six players.

Pitch and goals

The field for field hockey and the pitch for indoor hockey have specific measurements for sidelines, goal lines and circle lines.

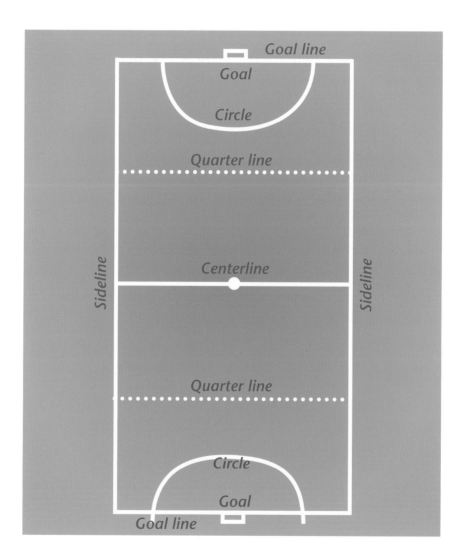

Children play on a smaller field. Most of the time, it's one half of a large field. Indoor hockey is played on a team handball court.

Age groups and playing time

Indoor hockey and field hockey games are played in two halves for all age groups.

		Field	Indoor
Boys/girls	U 10 (under 10)		
		2 x 25 minutes	2 x 10 minutes
Boys/girls	U 12 (under 12)		
Boys/girls	U 14 (under 14)	2 x 30 minutes	2 x 12 minutes
Youth	U 16 (under 16)		
Youth	U 18 (under 18)		
Seniors and adults	19 and older	2 x 35 minutes	2 x 15 minutes
			Up to 2 x 30 minutes

This is how the ball can be played

The ball can only be played with the flat side of the stick. The edge of the stick is also considered part of the flat side.

Field hockey:

- The ball can be pushed, hit, flicked and lifted.
- It should be played low.
- High passes must not endanger any player.
- Flicked and lifted balls are allowed as shots on goal.

Indoor hockey:

- The ball must be played low.
- The ball cannot be hit.
- Flicked and lifted balls as shots on goal are only allowed inside the circle.

When is a goal valid?

A goal is valid when:

- The shooter is inside the circle.
- The ball has completely crossed the goal line.

A goal is not valid when:

- The shooter stands outside the circle.
- The ball does not completely cross the goal line.

THE GAME

The kick-off

At the start of the game and after a goal, the ball is brought into the game from the center of the playing field. The players remain in their half of the playing field. They may cross the centerline immediately after the kick-off.

The bully

If the game has to be interrupted without a violation, play resumes where it left off. That must always be outside of the circle. For a bully two players stand facing each other. The flat side of the stick and the left shoulder point towards the opposing goal. All other players keep a distance of at least 5 meters (5 1/2 yards) in field hockey and 3 meters (3 1/4 yards) in indoor hockey.

This is how it's done:

The sticks first touch the ground on the right side of the ball and then the opposing sticks touch above the ball. This is done three consecutive times. After that, the ball can be played.

3 x

FAIRNESS COMES FIRST

Be fair to your opponent

You cannot play hockey without your sports partner. Or would you like to always shoot on an empty goal with no challenge? You should always treat your opponent with consideration and fairness.

Be fair to your teammates

Everyone is doing his best and no one makes a mistake deliberately. No one benefits from being yelled at and berated. Instead, help the weaker player so next time he will be better able to support the team.

Be honest

Be honest with yourself. When you don't reach a ball, play it out of bounds, or something isn't going as well as you'd like, don't blame someone else, but look to yourself for the mistake first. Play by the rules, even when the referee isn't looking.

Important rules for a fair game

There are a few very important rules for playing hockey. If everyone abides by them, the risk of injury is minimal and you will have lots of fun playing the game together.

- The ball should be played low. It should never travel so high that it injures a player.

- The stick only touches the ball and never the opponent.

- The hands hold the stick and never push, scratch, hit or pull the opponent's jersey.

- The feet should be fast and nimble, but should never kick or trip the opponent.

Playing a sport together, practicing and preparing for a game to win with the team – that's the best! At the same time you learn to value friendship, cooperation and camaraderie. Athletes play fair!

HEY! WHY DON'T YOU GUYS WANT TO PLAY ANYMORE?

CAN YOU GUESS WHY?

Take a close look at these players. What does not conform to regulations and is unfair play? What are they doing wrong?

1

2

3

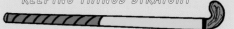

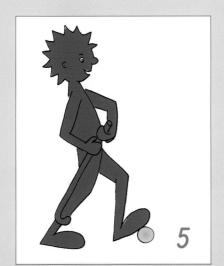

Do you know any other violations of the rules? Write them down here!

_____

_____

_____

THE REFEREE

It is important that an actual hockey game with goals, victory and defeat is umpired by a referee. He makes sure that all players play by the agreed rules. He is in charge and all players must accept his decisions. That also applies when you may have seen the situation differently and would have made a different decision yourself.

. . . . .9 LET'S PLAY

To play hockey in a park, on the street, in the schoolyard or elsewhere, you don't necessarily need two teams with 11 players each, two regulation size goals or a playing field with exact lines. Hockey is also lots of fun on a smaller field without lines and with a goal made from backpacks and gym bags. Besides, different playing opportunities are great for practicing your receiving and passing techniques, as well as your ball control and getting open.

Find a suitable place to play. Make sure that there is no  *threat of broken windows and trampled flowerbeds from errant balls. Avoid freshly painted surfaces and stay off heavily traveled streets. Got it? Have fun!*

A GAME WITH FRIENDS

The teams

You want to form teams but can't come to an agreement? Here is a tip: The two smallest players stand facing each other. They walk towards each other with "coffee beans," small steps where the heel is set against the toe of the other foot. Whoever is first to step on the other's toes gets to pick the first player for his team. Now you take turns until all players have been chosen.

The rules

Even if you are just playing with your friends in the park or in the schoolyard, some things have to be discussed. Make your own rules before the game starts.

- Who plays together on a team?

- Where are the goals? Is there a permanent goalie?

- Is there an "out of bounds" or do you keep playing?

- What constitutes a foul? When do you get a corner kick, a free kick or a bully?

Sometimes you only realize during the game that something was left unsettled. Talk about it! To avoid disagreements, you can also designate a teammate as referee.

If no coach, teacher or trainer is present, the players can set their own rules. Everyone has a voice! It is not the biggest, the strongest or the one who owns the ball that decides how to play.

A few tips from Elo:

- Be careful not to disturb anyone!

- Make sure no windows are broken, and no cars or flowerbeds are damaged!

- Look out for small children or people walking!

- Be mindful of newly built homes and freshly painted surfaces!

- Beware of street traffic!

- In the heat of the game, things can get pretty loud. Make sure the noise doesn't bother anyone!

- _____

- _____

- _____

THIS IS HOW YOU CAN PLAY

To have fun playing hockey, you don't necessarily need a pitch with artificial turf, lines and two goals. You also don't have to wait until you have enough players for two complete teams.

Look for a suitable place, agree on a few necessary rules, pick up your sticks and go!

We have used different symbols to illustrate the game ideas so you can understand them. Here you see an explanation of the symbols. It is called a *legend*.

●   ●   This is a goal.

▲   This is a player.
Players of the same team are the same color.

▲   This is an opposing player.
The opposing players are a different color.

——————   This is a marking line.

•••••••►   This line shows how the ball should be played.

1 **1:1**

You need two goals of equal size and a centerline. Each player stands in front of his goal. Now try to play the ball to the other side to score a goal. Of course, each player will want to protect his goal and stop the ball. The centerline cannot be crossed.

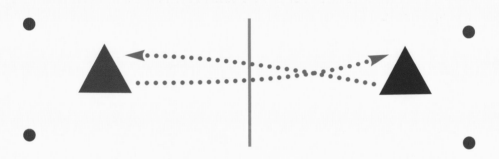

2 **2:2**

You need two goals of equal size and a centerline. Each team consists of two players who score goals and defend their goal. Each team stays on its half of the field and the centerline cannot be crossed. Also play the ball to your teammate until one of you is in a good position to take a shot.

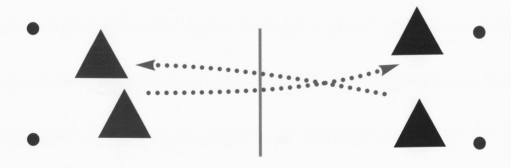

3 **3:3**

You play again like you did under number 2, only now there are three players on each team. But you can send the third player into the opposing half for interference.

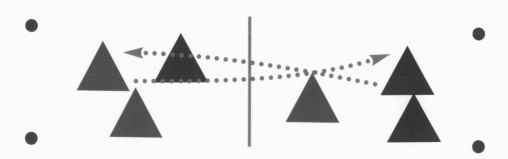

4 **Play with several goals**

Form two teams and set up several goals. A goal is scored when the ball rolls though the goal and is received on the other side by a member of one's own team.

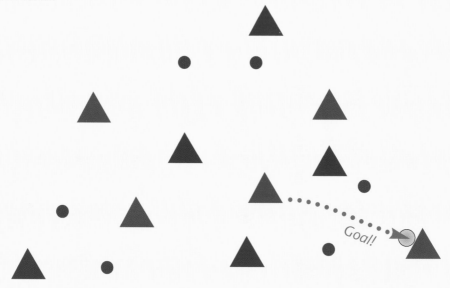

Goal!

5 Two teams and four goals

*Two teams play with four goals. Each team tries to score in the opponents'
two goals while simultaneously defending their own goals.*

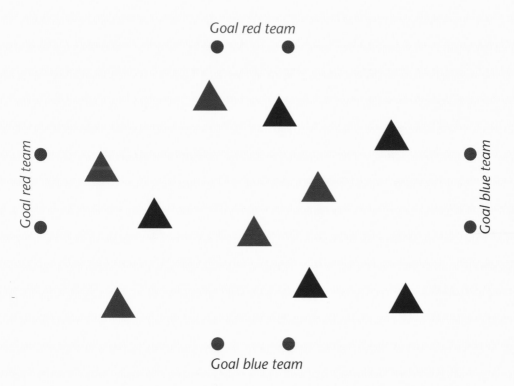

Even when playing with friends, make sure you:

- Get open so you can receive passes.
- With your teammates, try to get the highest score.
- Observe closely what the opponent is doing.

*Playing together should primarily be fun. But you can
certainly see that someone who plays a lot of hockey will
keep getting better. He improves the accuracy of his
passes, his ball control skills and his one-on-one prowess.*

. . . . .10 FIT AND HEALTHY

Most people who play sports want to have fun and suceed. But an additional important goal is keeping one's body fit and healthy.

EATING RIGHT

Someone who participates in sports, runs and jumps, uses up more energy than a couch potato. That is why food always tastes best after those practice sessions – because you are hungry and thirsty and have to replenish your energy supply.

Almost all children like to eat chocolate, chips, French fries, and pizza. But that's not the best food for athletes, particularly if you eat these things too frequently and in large quantities. These foods contain too much fat.

The better meal for an athlete consists of whole grain bread with cheese, fruit and yogurt. There are many foods that are healthy and taste good, too. Try to have a varied and moderate diet.

This athlete is really hungry after practice. He would like to just eat and drink everything at once. What would you recommend? Cross out anything that in your opinion is not very healthy!

Which food should you eat more frequently during the day, and when you need a snack? Cross out every L, Y, M, A, X, E, K and D.

F	D	K	A	R	E	X	Y	M	L	A
M	E	L	M	A	U	D	I	K	D	Y
Y	A	D	D	L	K	Y	M	A	M	T

IF YOU SWEAT, YOU HAVE TO DRINK REGULARLY

When you sweat during training and while playing, your gym clothes are often soaked and you can see the perspiration on your skin.

Sweating isn't bad – in fact, it's very healthy. But your body misses the fluids you lose when you sweat. That's when you have to drink a lot so your body once again has enough fluids.

Thirst quenchers

The best thirst quenchers are:

- Water

- Mineral water

- Water and juice mix

  (apple juice, orange juice or cherry juice diluted with water)

- Herbal tea or fruit tea (also sweetened with honey)

Pure juice and soft drinks are not suitable for replenishing fluids. They contain too much sugar.

When you are thirsty and drink, you have to be careful not to drink too hastily. It is better to take smaller sips more often. Be careful not to fill your stomach so full that you will barely be able to move.

OH BOY!
MY STOMACH IS SO FULL!
I JUST HAD A GIANT THIRST!

HELLO, DOCTOR!

"Hello, Doctor," is what you will cheerfully say to your doctor because as an athlete you usually feel fit all around. But even if you're not sick, you should see the doctor at least once a year for a checkup. Tell him that you play hockey. He will examine you and tell you whether you can train without concern.

Have your vaccination record checked and get some nutritional tips.

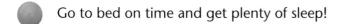

A successful day begins with a good start in the morning!

A few tips from Elo:

- Go to bed on time and get plenty of sleep!

- Look forward to the new day.

- Stretch after getting up. How about some morning calisthenics? On the following page, you will find some exercises.

- A cold shower is ideal after washing. It is refreshing and toughens you up.

- Whole grain bread, granola, cornflakes, milk, yogurt and fruit are all part of a good and healthy breakfast.

- Don't forget to brush your teeth after you eat!

Don't forget to warm up!

Your trainer should always allow for a warm-up at the beginning of a training session. It is important that your muscles become warm, loose and flexible through different exercises. That is how you protect yourself from injuries.

Even when you do activities at home or play with your friends, don't forget to warm up!

WARM-UP EXERCISES

To warm up, you can jog or do some easy jumping exercises.

Stretch really tall and stand on your toes at the same time, like you are trying to pick apples.

Now collapse suddenly and make yourself really small.

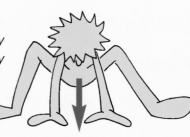

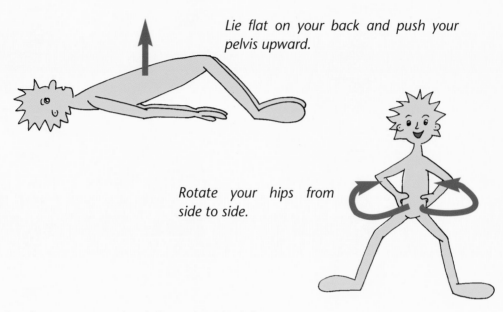

Lie flat on your back and push your pelvis upward.

Rotate your hips from side to side.

Bend your torso to the right and to the left.

Do you sometimes have problems getting going in the morning? These exercises are also well suited as morning calisthenics.

.....11 PLAYING FOR A CLUB

At some point, you will find that playing in the backyard, on the street or behind the house is no longer enough. That's when it is time to join a club. There you can play on a team, be a part of the action and participate in real competitions.

How do you find a club?

Find out if your parents will give their approval to your playing hockey for a club. If yes, find a sports club that offers hockey in your community or near your home.

If you are lucky, your friends or school buddies are already playing on a team and will take you along to their practice.

If you don't know where to find a club, look on the Internet under www.usfieldhockey.com.

Most of the time, sports clubs have an information desk or a bulletin board where telephone numbers or practice times are posted. Make an appointment to try out. Then you can take your time seeing how everything works. You can meet the trainer and the other children and you can see how they practice. Of course, everything will be new and strange at first. That's totally normal!

Usually you will be asked how old you are and which age group you belong in. That is how you are classified for a team in the club. It depends on your birth year and not what grade you are in.

Now you will try out for a club of your choice or participate in a practice session on a trial basis. Your parents, older siblings or grandparents should accompany you. Bring along gym clothes and athletic shoes.

If you like it and the trainer says you are suited for playing hockey, you should sign up. You will then become a member of the club and receive a membership card.

MY FIRST HOCKEY CLUB

My club is called: _____

Date I joined: _____

My trainers: _____

My team:
(Names, signatures)

Our team colors: _____

Our logo:

Keeping track of the game results is interesting and fun.
You can record them on this page.

Opponent/Date	Result

What does a club and team member have to do?

• Train diligently and perform well in games.
• Pay a monthly membership fee.
• Take care of the club's uniform and clothing.

What does the club have to do?

• Insure the athletes against sport-related accidents and injuries.
• Organize the training and game activities.
• Issue a player's pass to the member.
• Provide sticks, balls and goalie equipment for beginner training.
• Organize transportation to games.
• Provide trainers and coaches at the club.

Can I leave the club or change over to another club?

If you want to leave the club or change over to another club, you should cancel your membership in writing.

There sometimes can be a changeover ban or penalty.

Do I always have to go to practice?

• Punctuality and regularity are important rules in sports. Otherwise you won't learn anything.

• If you really can't make it to a practice session, try to let the trainer or coach know beforehand.

• If you are having problems with your academic performance, school has to come first. Discuss it with your trainer.

. . . . .12 SOLUTIONS

Pg. 10   **In the picture are:**
Basketball, volleyball, ping-pong, football, hockey, soccer, tennis.

Here is what else we thought of:
Baseball, team handball, rhythmic gymnastics, polo, water polo.

Pg. 16

| M | A | M | M | O | T | H |

P. 20   There are 17 balls on the two pages. Of these, sixteen are scattered about and one lies next to the mammoth.

Pg. 40   There are eight sticks in this pile.
Stick number **3** and stick number **8** are identical.

Pg. 52   1   B – shinny
2   D – guards
3   A – in a sports hall
4   C – a part of the stick

Pg. 60   Player number 1 plays the ball to his teammate.

Pg. 66/67 Mistakes the players are making with body and stick position.

1   The right hand is at the top and the left hand is at the bottom. It should be the reverse!

2   The hands are too close together. The left hand belongs at the top of the stick.

3   The player stands too erect. He won't be able to react quickly enough.

4   The arms are too close to the body. The stick is therefore too upright and not in a 45° position.

5   The player is not paying attention and is holding the stick too casually. He is therefore not ready to receive a pass and will take much too long to react.

Pg. 78/79 Mistakes the players are making with ball control.

1   The arms are too close to the body, making the stick position too vertical.

2   The stick is held with only one hand. There is no steady guidance.

3   The ball bounces up.

4   The stick comes up too high when switching from forehand to backhand.

5   The ball rolls between the feet, but it should be farther forward on the line.

6   The player stands too erect and too stiffly.

Pg. 88   Mistakes the players are making with the push pass.

1   The player stands too erect and his legs are not in a straddle position.

2   The stick is not held at a 45° angle but rather too close to the body.

3   There is no swing for the push pass like there is for a hit.

Pg. 89   **Mistakes the players are making when hitting.**

1   The player is not in a lateral position and stands too stiffly.
2   The player holds the stick in the middle rather than at the top. He therefore does not have enough power and momentum.
3   The stick is slowed down after the hit, but it should still follow the ball.

Pg. 90   Here is a way to get out of the maze.

Pg. 100/101   What will happen when the players make these mistakes while receiving the ball?

1   The ball will bounce off the stick to the front or to the side.
2   The ball will bounce over the stick.
3   The ball will roll under the stick.

Number 4, the bonus question:

The player is holding the stick upside down, meaning the head is at the top. That will hopefully never happen!

Pg. 104   Ela's stick is stick number 2.

Pg. 112/113   **Mistakes and rule violations**

1   The stick is used to play the ball and not to hold on to the opponent.

2   Even when you are angry, you don't just throw down your stick! It is unsportsmanlike and the risk of injury is too great!

3   Hitting is not allowed! Instead, trick the opponent with good technique.

4   There is no hitting, spitting or otherwise insulting or injuring the opponent.

5   Only the goalie is allowed to stop the ball with his foot or hold on to it.

6   All players should treat the referee with respect. Insults are unsportsmanlike and will be punished.

Pg. 124

F	D	K	A	R	E	X	Y	M	L	A
M	E	L	M	A	U	D	I	K	D	Y
Y	A	D	D	L	K	Y	M	A	M	T

. . . . .13 LET'S TALK

If this were a book for adults, these pages for the parents and trainers would of course appear at the very front of the book as the preface. But since it is a book for children we are putting this chapter at the end, sort of as an addendum.

Our beginning hockey players are mostly elementary school students who have just learned to read and have not yet had very much exposure to books. They are absolutely in need of support from adults who can help them with the approach to the book. The best way to start is by leafing through the book, looking at the pictures, filling in the questionnaires and recording personal information. This book does not have to be read back to back, but is also very useful as a reference work and diary.

Have fun reading together!

Do you remember the first time your little son or daughter chased after a ball and wanted to play with it? Maybe you'll say: As soon as my child was able to walk! Your child never lost this fascination with the ball and has chosen one of many ball sports. He or she wants to learn to play hockey, maybe even practice at a club with experienced coaches and well-trained trainers. It is great that you want to support him or her in learning this appealing sport.

Hockey is a sport for boys, as well as for girls. Aside from the indoor season the games are always outside on the field and thus in the fresh air. Hockey can be learned as early as pre-school age, and once the first basic elements have been learned, there will be exciting plays and the first goals. Hockey distinguishes itself through its diversity of movements, is demanding in terms of technique, general skillfulness, and endurance, and it promotes concentration and quick decision making.

One advantage is that skillful stick control allows the somewhat physically weaker players to also achieve successes. Your child is part of a social community and learns the specifics of team play, as well as the importance of the individual player. Each player learns to persevere and to deal with success and failure at games.

Personal responsibility must be learned, too. By and by the players take responsibility for the care and completeness of the equipment and pay attention to punctuality and regularity in training and competition. So be supportive of your child's desire to play hockey, practicing and training.

In the beginning, the enjoyment of playing, of the movement, the dribbling and scoring goals in the various forms of play is prevalent with our little players. Of course, this does require some basic technique, but that should not be the main focus just yet. The children should play, have fun, and in doing so develop their skills. That is also our wish with this book. Besides the explanations of necessary basic technique and hockey rules, the children also learn a lot about the game of hockey in general. They have the opportunity to become actively involved in their favorite sport.

Be helpful, but with prudence and patience!

Do not allow your expectations for your child to get too high. What matters most is the enjoyment of the sport and playing. Excessive ambition would only be harmful. Don't compare your child to others of the same age because biological development, particularly at this age, can vary greatly. Just focus on your own child and praise his or her progress. Your child will thank you.

Support from hockey parents

Parental support is in demand in hockey, too. Be it for the organization of training attire, rides to the field or to games, Mom or Dad, or even Grandma or Grandpa have to be available as partners for playing and practicing. When your child is part of a team, some of your weekends will be affected by the playing activities. If a game is scheduled for Saturday or Sunday, the family has breakfast early, the parents are

chauffeurs for part of the team, and the siblings want to come along to cheer. Sunday dinner has to wait until the whistle blows, and visits to Grandma's are only planned for days without games.

But what's better than seeing your own eager little player be irrepressibly happy about scoring his first goal? Or how much trust and intimacy parents and children experience when a defeat requires comforting. Be glad that your child is getting regular exercise, regardless of whether your child will become an internationally successful super-player or is "only" enjoying the game and the camaraderie.

And one more thing:

Savor the game and enjoy the actions of the little players. Children are unnerved by parents shouting during a game. The children need to make their own decisions, and technical suggestions, as well as substitutions, are the trainer's responsibility.

By the way:

Many clubs offer "parents hockey." Here, parents can play regardless of whether they have played before or are total beginners!

What a children's hockey trainer should have:

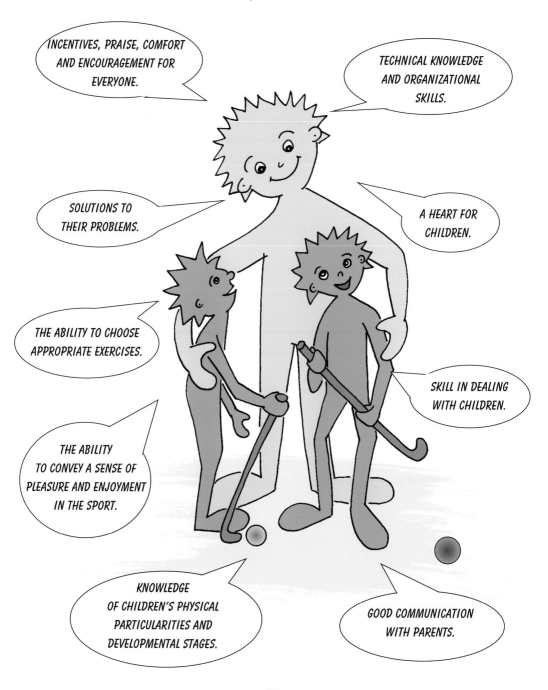

DEAR HOCKEY TRAINER,

Surely you'll agree that it is a great feeling to see these little guys with their excited faces and expectant eyes. Now it is up to you to introduce them to hockey.

But all children are different. There are the self-confident ones and the timid ones, the diligent and the not-so-diligent, the talented and the less talented. Each child has its own little personality with individual qualifications and his own developmental history, with hopes and desires, feelings and needs. Children want to be active, to move and have fun. Particularly in a group, they are able to match themselves with their peers and spur each other on.

A beginning hockey player's most important role model is his coach or trainer. They watch everything very closely: How he talks to them, how he handles the stick and carries out the movements. They also pay close attention to how well their trainer adheres to the rules and safety regulations.

The young player himself is the most important factor in the teaching and learning process. The child, no matter how young and how much of a beginner he may be, is always subject to his own development and is never just the object of our influence. Therefore, offer him sufficient tips and opportunities for his own development. Foster and utilize your little beginning hockey player's independence. Take the path from directing to inspiring. The children don't "have to" and aren't "supposed to," but they "can" and they "may."

The value of this little book

The value of this little book will depend entirely on how you will integrate it into the instruction. It is written specifically for children who are beginning hockey players. But it can also be recommended to parents who wish to accompany their child on this path.

The book focuses on the children's needs and is intended to help them engage in hockey away from the hockey field, as well. The child will acquire a fairly complete foundation for practicing via the book's illustrations and descriptions.

He will be better able to follow your explanations and demonstrations. The young players can review at their leisure what they have learned, keep track of goals and learning progress, and receive suggestions for practicing at home and with other children. This develops the ability to act independently and accelerates the learning process

An environment is created in which the children themselves, step by step, think about their practicing and learning, their movements, actions, and finally monitor and evaluate their behavior. They become a partner with the coaches and trainers. We would like the children to enjoy coming to practice and go home with a sense of achievement. And, of course, that would make the practice sessions fun for the trainer, as well.

The book and training

Tell the children that this book will be their personal companion while they learn to play hockey. Give them the logo of the club and take a photo to paste in the book. This will boost their attachment to you, to the team and the club.

Help the children to use this book properly. In the beginning, read some segments together and explain to the children how the photos

and illustrations should be viewed and understood. Together, with the little players, make entries regarding goals, suggestions, etc. In doing so, you create critical orientation guides for their understanding and independent practicing.

With the aid of this book, you can also assign homework for the next training session. The children read up on a topic and get to do a show-and-tell at the next session.

We always welcome suggestions and additions.

We wish you and your little protégées lots of fun and enjoyment, and, of course, athletic successes, too.

PHOTO & ILLUSTRATION CREDITS:

Cover design: Jens Vogelsang, Aachen
Illustrations: Katrin Barth
Cover photo: Wolfgang Quednau
Photos (inside): Berndt Barth, Herbert Bohlscheid, direvi, Wolfgang Quednau, Ulrike Sluga

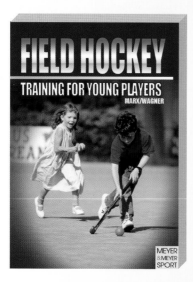

Marx/Wagner
Field Hockey Training
for Young Players

2nd edition
160 pages, two-color print
226 photos, 204 figures
Paperback, 5^3/4" x 8^1/4"
ISBN 1-84126-136-X
£ 12.95 UK/$ 17.95 US
$ 25.95 CDN/€ 16.90

The Book

Five game situations show the correct way to play. Starting point is the basic thought of scoring a goal or preventing a goal being scored. In this way one begins to play hockey from the word go. Playing the game is always taken as the central point for discussion and is complemented by a large selection of games and exercises, tips abaout tactics, precise descriptions regarding movement and actions, correcting faults as well as a successive build-up of the rules of the game. This revised edition of the book is designed in the first instance for trainers and coaches – even those without any experience of field-hockey – students, exercise leaders and club trainers in the school and youth sectors.

MEYER
& MEYER
SPORT

MEYER & MEYER distribution@m-m-sports.com • www.m-m-sports.com